Comments about the author and her works.

Write Again. Isaac Osagie, RCCG, Calabar.

Inspiring writer with a definite flow. David Wong, MTI, Malaysia.

A constant read. Can't put her books down easily. Gbemi Fayose, London.

Found her book in Scotland, a treasure to the owner. Emmanuel Ogbeche, DA, Portharcourt.

The women need her book. Simeon Afolabi, RPA, Portharcourt

I trip for the book. Kunle Olawale, RCCG, Lagos.

A captivating read with a superb flow. Keep writing, don't stop. Ekong Udoh MD, IBC, Calabar.

A much sought-after writer. Her books lift, inspire, edify. Ukeme Obot, TACS-FON, Calabar.

Compelling story-telling skills, thought-provoking, entertaining, creative and pastoral. A writer to watch. Eddie Tah Offre, HCC, Calabar.

Arresting, ingenious, compelling. Kammonke Abam, Splendour Magazine.

A very good book. Lady Dorothy Tunde-Adeleye, AC, Calabar.

Uplifting, refreshingly different. Sasi Miet Jaja, Eklesia Magazine.

Unique approach. Fred Abua, RBC, Calabar.

Can't drop till you finish. Regina Gbemudu, RCCG, Lagos.

Highly recommended for every woman. Amanda Andersen, NWIM, Tenesee, U.S.A.

Beautiful book. Austin Mboso, Springhouse, Calabar.

A blessing to the lives of women. Blessing Okon, WC, Ikot-Ekpene.

Good book, difficult to drop. Kehinde Jokosenumi, VLM, Ilesa.

The women in South Africa are hungry for her books. Shadrach Pandala, ALMC, South Africa.

A great treasure, a source of tremendous blessing. Funke Joseph, RCCG, Lagos.

An author, worthy of note. Lady Courage, NHFC, Philadelphia, U.S.A.

The Devil Lied

Sex lies taken to be truth

Sinmisola Ogúnyinka

Cover Design by Amazingrafiks © 2007

Contents

My mother, Mrs. Tinuola Ifaturoti, and grandmother Mrs. Frances Majekodunmi both preserved the pride in remaining pure in their marriage beds and taught me to beware of the devil's sex lies, saving me from countless evils borne out of falling prey to the devil.

Author's Note

I want to thank God for putting this book together. I desire sincerely that this book will minister to parents and children alike.

The essence is to challenge every Christian to face the lies the devil has been telling and to shame him at his own tricks. When we take up this challenge, we affect our lives and those of our loved ones for good; affect the church of God for good, thereby affecting the society for good. We preach the word and win souls for Christ by being examples, and we defeat the devil. How wonderful.

I recommend this book for parents, guardians, and adults generally, and most especially for youths and children from age seven. The slogan is: CATCH THEM YOUNG!

May God give us depth and understanding in Jesus' name. Amen.

FACT SHEET

I t is important to give this book a very fundamental and practical beginning. For this reason, we will look at some definitions and facts about our physical growth and what gives birth to self-consciousness and need.

It will be expedient to note that sometime in our lives, we were all youths, and some lies that we heard then, have followed us into adulthood and held us bound.

ORIGIN OF LIES

Lies originated even before the foundation of the world. The devil is a master at telling lies. Before Genesis chapter 1, there was war in heaven based on a lie. The devil assumed he could rule better than God, and convinced himself to believe this lie! And then he convinced one third of the angels in heaven to follow him, of course, he made them believe that lie too Isaiah 14:12-14, Ezekiel 28:11-17, Revelations 12:7-12. After God created the world, positioning the first man and woman to rule, the old liar came back with his tricks and told the first lie man was ever accosted with, to Eve Genesis 3. Just as we see the repercussion of lies in the Bible times, we still see it today. Every lie believed and acted out yields results.

WHAT IS ADOLESCENCE?

Adolescence is the age of the beginning of awareness and it is divided into three. The early adolescence (age 10 - 11), begins with a burst of biological changes that evokes alien feelings of anxiety, bewilderment and delight. At this stage, in both sexes, there are evidential changes in body growths, especially in the chest region, and the limbs. At this stage also, there is an increase in the sex hormones which results in hair growths, enlargement and other physical developments. This period lasts for three to four years and it is this period that most normal girls experience menarche and most normal boys experience their first ejaculation. These changes have social and psychological implications and we often see these young adolescents feeling awkward, self conscious, dissatisfied with their physical appearances and often embarrassed by unexpected sexual urges. When I was 11 years old, I had a 'ridiculous' crush for a boy in my class and had fantasies about the two of us. I also had the 'privilege' of witnessing two of my form 1 female classmates having a physical 'combat' over a boy that was also our classmate, while everyone watched and cheered!

The second stage of the adolescent is known as middle adolescence. This stage records the adolescent, having seen the changes, making moves to adapt and make the best out of him/herself. This period usually starts from 14 years and it is the heat period of what psychologists refer to as 'teenage blues'. The adolescent seeks to break off from parental ties, often criticizing bitterly, parental standards despite the fact that they are majorly financed by their parents. Sexual urges become more intense at this stage, especially in boys and due to a need to preserve a self-image among peers, satisfaction for this urge is usually pursued. In a bid to establish his/her identity, the adolescent often seeks love and acceptance through sex. This period also lasts about four years.

The late adolescence is the last stage and this includes the late teens and early twenties. Neither child nor adult, the adolescent is faced with the task of blending with society, taking responsibilities and facing the challenges of early adulthood.

Until we understand the need for every young person to answer the questions of identity, purpose, and pursuit, we may not be able to accept that the devil tells lies to our youths, and the youths take these lies to be truth. May God help us in Jesus' mighty name. Amen.

Chapter 1 - IN THE BEGINNING

" ... So God created man in His own image, in the image of God He created him; male and female he created them Gen.1:27..."

When God finished creation, He saw that what He had created was good. And God told Adam to name all the animals of the earth and whatever he (Adam) named, God put a seal on Gen.2:19-20, but God realized He had unfinished work. The woman was still inside Adam! So He caused Adam to sleep and brought out Eve. When Adam saw Eve, however, we may want to interpret this scripture, the truth is that Adam acknowledged what God had done for him as he stated in Gen.2:23. He appreciated and loved Eve, and the two were naked but were not ashamed Gen.2:25.

In the beginning, there was purity and there was perfection ...until sin came and polluted man Genesis 3. From then on, the perversion keeps increasing. The bible says that hell has enlarged its mouth Isaiah 5:14.

God invented sex from the beginning. He designed the hormones that trigger your desires. He designed every nerve ending that magnifies pleasure. He designed sex as a good gift from Him because He loves us and wants us to be happy. However good God's intensions were, they were not to be perverted and God gave strict instructions for the use of this good gift. Specifically, it was meant for the 'Man and his wife' Gen. 2:23-25. One man with one woman within the legal bounds of marriage. It wasn't meant for a girl and her female friend, or a boy and his male friend. It wasn't meant for you alone to stimulate yourself and it wasn't meant for you and as many people as you like. Sex is not just physical. It is spiritual and it is bonding.

Deliverance ministers all over the world agree that sex is one of the most potent ways of transferring spirits. It is not just body contact, it is life transference. Countless ministers have lost their anointing because of infidelity. Businesses have crashed, marriages ruined, ministries scattered and countless unmentionable destruction wrought due to illicit sex.

It's time to confront the lies the devil has been telling our youths, and blow them up in his face. Amen. The book of Proverbs is quite vocal about the evils of illicit sex, especially in Proverbs 2 and 7. Stolen waters is sweet Prov. 9:17, and thus we find ourselves falling continually into the sins associated with sex. The bible refers to this sin as very unique and especially 'disgusting' in the sight of God because it is committed in and on our bodies which is the temple of the living God I Cor. 6:18-19. We must understand that God desires that we be clean and pure, holy and acceptable in His sight, which is our reasonable service Romans 12:1. An illustration that comes readily is the one my English teacher once gave while I was in Senior Secondary 3 (SS3). He told us that supposing we asked our younger sister to bring water for us, and the girl gets a clean glass, puts clean water, and suddenly as she is about to hand it over, a fly drops inside the water or some dirt, drops in, would we still drink it? Obviously, the answer is No. If this sister carries a dirty glass and pours clean water, would we drink? No. If she pours dirty water into a clean glass, would we drink? No.

Sex before marriage and outside the context of 'man and his wife' is dirt in our lives. When God looks into the glass and sees even an iota of dirt, he throws the whole lot out. May we not be thrown out in Jesus' name. Amen. In subsequent chapters, we will see some of the excuses that we give for doing what we do, which is very wrong before God. Rom. 2:1a says thou art inexcusable, O man. Others have gone before us, faced temptations such as ours and have been able to overcome. I Cor. 10-13 say that there is no temptation that has come to us for which God will not make a way of escape. It applies to every aspect of our lives. However, because the devil has told lies that we believe, we fall, without even knowing we have fallen. In this book we will read of testimonies of men and women who have kept themselves for their spouses, and thanked God for it. It is more honorable before God and before man to keep the marriage honorable and the bed undefiled Hebrews 13:4.

It is never too late to go back to God's original plan. Acts 17:30 says that the days of ignorance, God winked at. The devil knows that sins committed with our bodies are the most difficult to forget so he gives us all the reasons why we should commit this sin. Brothers and Sisters, I want to admonish that we can 'live above sin'. It is possible. May the Lord open our eyes and give us the strength to do what is right in His sight. James 4:17 says if we know

to do good, and we do it not, then we have
sinned.

Chapter 2 - OLD LIES

The Lie: Sex is love

Sex is not love. I love you does not mean I should have sex with you.

Abel and Tania were the perfect couple-to-be. She was the fellowship's treasurer and he was in charge of Sunday School. These were the ideal two - the couple made in heaven.

Brothers and sisters alike looked up to them and even emulated them. However, there was an attraction that was between them, that neither could control. Abel knew he loved her deeply like his own flesh but could not understand why his body reacted to her the way it did. He had never known a woman in his life and had always avoided 'X- rated' stuff. The deep feeling was also true for Tania. Tania had told him she had sexual relationships with two different men before she gave her life to Christ, and he had accepted that as part of what may be totally unavoidable. Afterall, we were all new creatures in Christ and old things had passed away, he consoled himself and assured her. However, when he realized his emotions were beginning to get out of hand, he spoke out to Tania.

At first, his complaint came as a mere protest and rebuke for his unholy desires. When she however confirmed the feelings she also had, he decided they had to do something about it. They both agreed they had to find a way of easing off the 'tension'. It started as a hug and a kiss. For him it was a totally new experience. A totally new experience he came to welcome and look forward to. After all, he loved her and he needed to express it. Gradually, they both independently gave reasons why they needed to express the 'love' more and more to themselves. The first reason was the deep love they had for each other and the desire to please each other. The second reason was the promise to marry one another in the nearest possible time and a third reason was the need to have a release 'so that they could concentrate' on the things of God. They completely missed the true definition of love as it is in 1Cor.13. One evening, as they were together alone in his apartment, watching a documentary, her beauty overwhelmed him and he pulled her into his arms. They simply felt a need to feel each other. Suddenly there was a power outage. Darkness enveloped them and they remained locked in each other's arms, neither eager to break the serenity. He whispered his love for her and she whispered back affectionately. When he started to caress her, a little more intensely than ever before, she did not stop him. A few minutes later when power was restored, they were both half-naked but couldn't be bothered. That night Abel and Tania had their fill of 'love'! It was the first of many others. They both used preventives to caution themselves. They both told themselves they loved each other.

They both told themselves it was right. Tania found herself 'loving' Abel more. He was so strong, and active and fun though his teachings had become shallow and empty to her. Abel to his sudden realization also felt being used. He no longer felt comfortable reading the Bible, how much more preparing Sunday school outlines and teaching the word of God and he also began to realize Tania craved intimacy more than fellowship. He told himself he had to stop having sex with Tania. To cap it all up, the sexual urges he had for Tania began to supercede the respect he had for her person. One day, after a 'troubled' session of lovemaking, Abel called the relationship off. He told Tania sincerely, that he could not bear to look her in the face, and palpably accused her of seducing him and luring him into sin. The most upsetting part was that Tania felt just as bad and full of accusations. They had a gruesome quarrel that brought their courtship to a 'rude' end.

Sex is one of the many ways of expressing love, within the legal boundaries of marriage. However, many youths have come to believe that this is an old fashioned belief. The truth is that from the foundation of the world, the devil has used this lie to confuse people. We all seem to refer to the good old days but even in those good old days, there was sexual perversion. Sexual perversion is as old as the world because the bible is very vocal and explicit about sexual sin Genesis 19:30-38, 2 Samuel 13:1-16. It is true that in those days, sex was a taboo discussion but this does not in anyway reduce the extent to which it ate into the societal morals. These days, we consider that the society is more corrupt only because people have become increasingly more vocal about the issue of sex. Most especially in the western and first world countries, sex has become an every day issue and perversion of it is no longer a big deal. This is sad.

THE TRUTH

There are three broad definitions of love:

Erotic love from the Greek word Eros, is love characterized by intense, emotional attachment and powerful sexual feelings or desire. Outside the context of marriage, erotic love is destructive. It is this kind of love that the devil defines as sex. Before marriage, erotic love should be suppressed continually and determinedly and even after marriage it should be geared only towards our marriage partner. In chapter six you will find guidelines on how to suppress and guide this love so that it will not separate us from God, and those we sincerely love. The kind of love the devil characterizes as sex is actually lust. Lust is the desire to excessively gratify our selfish desire transferred through the natural senses. Lust could be for sex, power, money or any other thing. Sexual lust is what the devil tells us is love. The story of Amnon and Tamar explains fully this lie of the devil 2 Samuel 13. We must watch out that we do not fall into this trap of the devil.

Philia is philanthropic love or brotherly love that we have for our fellow human beings. It is friendship and compassion. This love motivates us to show kindness towards others, those we know and sometimes those who are less privileged, whom we do not know. Basically, it is what we feel towards those we are acquainted with, especially in the church of God Hebrews 13:1. Believers and unbelievers alike can operate this kind of love freely and easily as it is natural love. An example of this love is found between David and Jonathan I Samuel 18:3.

Agape is the third and purest kind of love. It is the giving love; God's kind of love - 'chaste, patient and undemanding'. Agape love motivates us to give unendingly and unceasingly. This love is the only kind of love that can enable us to 'turn the other cheek' Matthew 5:39. This is also the love that motivated God to give His only son as sacrifice for us John 3:16. Only believers in Christ have the ability to demonstrate this love. 1Corinthians 13 talks about Agape.

We must note that any time the word 'love' is used, we must sincerely search ourselves to know what kind of 'love' we are feeling, so that the devil will not confuse us. When your fiancé/fiancée says they want to express their deep love for you by having sex with you, you must flee. It is not love. It is lust. It is sin. It will destroy the real love (Agape), and probably destroy you! God wants us to be wise and sensitive and do that which is right in His sight.

The Lie: Everyone is doing it

No. Not everyone is having premarital sex. Sex before marriage is a sin. We were made to believe that a man must have sex with several people before marriage so that he will be able to satisfy his wife and vice versa but these are not true. A dear sister and friend got confused when her old, unmarried aunt advised her to make sure to have sex before marriage, otherwise, no man would want her when she told them she was a virgin. I screamed when she told me and asked for my advise! I'll throw the question to our Christian brothers – As a genuine, spirit-led, child of God, would you prefer to marry a brand new virgin or a refurbished virgin?

Phillip had battled with the urges he was having for such a long time. As a Christian, he
knew that sex before marriage was wrong yet,
he couldn't seem to control his desires. He had
prayed about it, and told himself he would
remain a virgin till marriage. Initially, it was
easy for him since he wasn't into any relationship. However, after he met Sarah, he realized
the battle line had been drawn. His friends
encouraged him to date her and he went ahead
and did. It started as a merely casual relationship. They went to a concert and then had a
drink. They were both students and had met
in the Youth Fellowship Love Feast organized
in their Church. Sex was not an issue at first
but as 'love' began to grow between him and
Sarah; Phillip took the advice of his friends.
Incidentally he was the only virgin amongst
them. They encouraged him to try sex with
Sarah. At first he thought she would refuse,

being a Christian. To his surprise, she was willing. After a few months of 'dating and sleeping' with Sarah, the attraction diminished and they 'fell out' with one another.

Phillip dated other sisters after Sarah, and somehow, they all ended up in his bed. Then he met Christie. Christie was a virgin. Phillip saw in her the true 'wife material' that he craved and for the first time since he started having relationships with ladies, he truly felt he should settle down. Besides, he had had years of 'fun' and marriage finally seemed appealing. Christie was a student and though he was working, and much older than her, he pursued the relationship. As usual, he started to date her. Christie responded only as she had with other suitors - with caution. He bought gifts for her, took her to programmes, gave her lots of attention, and even offered to drop her off at School once in a while. Christie liked him, and respected him... and watched him. Believing that the law 'not to fornicate' was no longer meant for believers, Phillip made advances at Christie. The first time he tried to kiss her as he dropped her off after a special anointing service in Church, Christie politely refused. She told him she didn't know him well enough. When he tried to do it again after two months, she slapped him and told him she never wanted to have anything to do with him again. Phillip lost out on marrying one of the most decent and beautiful Christians he could get, only because he believed everyone broke the heart of God like he did.

THE TRUTH

A remnant has been preserved to testify to the fact that not everyone is defiling him/herself. I read the 'Life Way' magazine vol. 3 No. 2, April-May, 2003 edition, and I was thrilled that some virgins, male and female, had come out even up to the extent of having their photographs featured, to share their testimonies. These are not twelve and thirteen year olds; they are successful young men and women, professionals, university and higher institution students, all of them 'beautiful' and 'handsome', sharing their stories with confidence and conviction. No one can convince me that it is old-fashioned to be chaste. Please don't allow the devil to convince you either.

It is beautiful to be chaste. It is decent to be chaste. It is Godly to be chaste. And it is not everyone that is being defiled. You too can be one of the desired remnants of the Lord. Even as Christians, some of us find it awkward to disclose that we are virgins. A friend of mine, a handsome, young, prospective business man and lawyer is 31 years old. He told me he is still a virgin and I believed him. Another male friend of mine, a 26 years old student of University of Calabar, told me he is a virgin I believe him. I got married as a virgin three years after graduation. My mother got married as a virgin and her own mother before her. Decent and orderly, educated and enlightened people also keep themselves. People who keep themselves are not weirdoes so don't let the devil confuse you that they are. To challenge us the more, my husband was also a virgin when we got married. What a sweet coincidence. The devil has so poisoned our minds that we believe it is shameful and an awkward thing to remain as a virgin. It is not. A sister and friend of mine told me that she wished she could have her past back. As a young Christian, she had foolishly yielded herself to having sex with her fiancé. The relationship became so riddled with guilt that she broke up with him after having an abortion. One sin led to another. When she learnt about this book project, she told me about her own regrets. She really wished she were still a virgin. She wants to help virgins like you keep your pride. May you have the strength to do so in Jesus' name. Amen.

The Lie: You will not enjoy sex in marriage

Foul! A close associate of mine, a born-again Christian, once told me she had vowed not to marry a virgin. She did not want to waste time 'learning' the art. She wanted a 'pro' who would readily please her. I couldn't understand her reasoning. She had definitely been confused by this foul lie of the devil.

A Christian couple I respected so much told me before I got married that there was nothing in sex. It was no big deal, and nothing to write home about! It kept me wondering and confused and guessing. They also confessed that the husband had been wild before he got born-again, which was before they got married. I sensed their marriage 'bed' was far from sweet and confirmed this a few weeks later when the man tried to fondle me in the secrecy of my one room apartment! I never opened my door to him again after God delivered me that day!

Sean had started having sexual relations as a young boy. When he was eleven years, he had followed his older brothers to a party and had sex with a sixteen year old girl. From then, it had been years of endless 'partying' and 'fornicating'. He later got born-again at the age of twenty-eight, and got married to Patricia when he was thirty-five. For the seven years between his re-birth and marriage, Sean struggled hard to keep himself. He stumbled twice. Marriage to Patricia hence, was a welcome relief. Sean, who had boasted that he was a 'reformed and regenerated male prostitute', however found sex with Patricia grossly unsatisfactory. It dawned on him that he had married her basically because she had had sexual relations before as an unbeliever. He had told himself he wouldn't have the patience to start afresh with a virgin! What a very wrong reason to marry a woman. She complained about the 'styles' he liked, and he complained about the 'styles' she knew. It wasn't long after their marriage before Sean sought shelter in the arms of other women - believers and unbelievers. His first purpose for marriage had failed. The marriage hit the rocks two years after when Sean got wind that his wife had been cheating as much as he had. Only God saved the marriage as the Church marriage committee intervened and the Pastor took them through series of re-orientation and prayers.

THE TRUTH

Sex does not require teaching or experience. The ability to enjoy sex is in-built. It is spontaneous. It is God-given. Most people that did not have sex before marriage will easily testify to the fact that this third lie of the devil is a big one. Solomon a great man of wisdom, married 300 women, and then got himself 700 concubines. If his appetite had been satisfied through practice, perhaps he would have stopped earlier. I stand to be corrected but most people that had premarital sex, enter marriage, not expecting much. Premarital sex is not a guarantee that sex in marriage will be good. In fact, many times, it is a guarantee that there will be dissatisfaction and infidelity. Instead of practicing sex before marriage, I highly recommend reading useful and Godly literature, attending marriage seminars and counseling that will educate us about sex without necessarily endangering or luring us into perversion. The confusion here is that we don't talk about sex. Youths from Christian homes or strict backgrounds are made to believe sex is bad. Parents tell their little children to 'shut your eyes' when watching a film with intimate moments. Sex talk is taboo. Youths want to know but they are criticized for seeking knowledge openly so they seek to practice secretly. They also watch blue movies and base their expectations on what they watch.

It is important to state here that sex on T.V is different from real sex in real life. Sex on T.V is practiced and acted. It may interest you to know that it is not spontaneous. The director tells them to maintain angles, and pace, to keep it up or low, make sounds or keep quiet. It is all make-believe and it is not real. When we base our expectations on such screen stuff, we miss it. We miss the fun because we feel our partner is not good enough. This is dangerous and could lead to infidelity. Jumping from partner to partner, looking for the real thing that actually took many 'heads' (directors, photographers, actors & actresses, etc.) to put together on screen.

If someone tells you that he/she got married as a virgin, and afterwards did not enjoy sex, something else may be responsible, not chastity before marriage. Perhaps the person was sexually abused as a child or wrongly taught and made to believe from childhood that sex is evil and dirty. If this person is a girl, has she been circumcised? All these and more add up to create emotional attitudes that handicap sexual adjustments in marriage. It is not the lack of sex before marriage that is responsible.

A dear friend of mine chided me for not telling her how 'sweet' marriage was a few days

after she got married. She had kept herself
till marriage. I told her that I had hinted her,
by insistently encouraging her to keep herself
chaste to her marriage bed. Sex is sweet when
you are both just discovering yourselves. It is
exciting when you depend on the Holy Spirit
to teach you what to do in 'bed' with your
spouse. And guess what, He does TEACH
even in that aspect!

Premarital sex breeds suspicion and fear.
Fear that someone else did it better. And some
of us just never seem to be able to get rid of the
'onions and garlic of Egypt' (Numbers 11:5)
even though we are headed for the 'promise
land'. May God show us mercy and give us
strength to over come in Jesus' mighty name.
Amen.

▼

The Lie: Sex is evil

This is a generational lie that the devil has
used to manipulate the counsel of parents and

guardians to their wards. Girls through the decades have been warned by their mothers not to allow a boy to 'touch' them as part of the orientation to starting their menstrual period. We all were told the same thing. Some parents go as far as telling their children that 'sex is evil'. I have even heard the school of thought that calls sex 'the forbidden fruit', the one that Eve ate in the Garden of Eden, and hence separated mankind from God. Whatever the case, the devil has obviously not left any stone unturned. While making some believe they can't do without it, he is making others dread the very thought of it! Harm can come to children who have been brainwashed into believing that sex is bad or wrong! While some parents label sex and related issues as no-go discussions, few who dare mention it paint it wrongly as something that should be feared and avoided. Many children have grown from this background into homosexualism and lesbianism. Some become frigid and cold from the fear of men and sex, in their matrimonial homes.

Gina came from a very strict Christian family. Sex talk was taboo. Like most young ladies, she was told as soon as she started her menstrual period, 'not to allow boys to touch her'. She adhered strictly to it. As she reached her late teens, pressure mounted on her from young men who were interested in her, but the words of her mother rang in her head.

"If you let a boy touch you, you will get pregnant, and your life will be ruined forever, your father will disown you!" Gina had asked then if it was really wrong to have children. Her thirteen-year-old mind had been confused about her mother's warning. She had always thought having children was a good thing, and one had to be pregnant first. "But Mummy," she asked, "isn't it good to have children?"

"Won't you let a boy touch you first before you have children?" her mother snapped. "Ngwanu! Go ahead and be having children. Silly girl"

The conversation had ended there. It took Gina one more year before she really got her thought sorted out and her mother's warning understood. But as pressure mounted from boys, so also did Gina struggle with what the truth really was. Her friends told her sex was cool. Boys can touch you all the time and you didn't have to get pregnant. Torn between her mother, friends, and suitors, Gina withdrew herself completely. She hated herself because her friends had begun to view her as a weirdo, and she had no confidence

in herself. She had been scared so much about sex and its relations that she grew gradually into a very confused young adult. Like most other things organised by her parents, Gina got married to a suitor approved by her parents. But the wedding night was far from fun for both newlyweds. It was the beginning of sex education for the confused adult. That first night, the couple did not consummate their marriage because Gina still believed it was wrong. Neither did they through the first week. When they finally did, Gina's husband had forced his wife and the ordeal had ended in a nightmare which further furnished poor Gina with the lie she had been fed from her youth, that sex is wrong!

Gina's story vaguely resembles that of a friend's. Though my friend allowed her husband to enjoy himself from their wedding night, it was just that! HE ENJOYED HIMSELF. My friend confided in me that she strongly believed sex was evil, and meant only for procreation. She never got to enjoy sex in her marriage through the three years I had been acquainted with her. Interestingly, she had not gotten this impression from parents but from her own sense of self-righteousness.

She said the belief that sex was evil had kept her from defiling herself as a single lady. It had worked. But the devil had made sure he used this fear of sex to hold her in bondage so that even after marriage, she was not free to enjoy sex.

THE TRUTH

The fear of sex is only the beginning of marital frustration, and nothing more. Rather, we should fear God, and delight in keeping His commandments. Blanket ban on sex and sex-related matters harm rather than help children. They may grow up believing that sex is actually bad. Well, it is not. What is bad is premature, premarital or indiscriminate sex. Abstaining from sex for the wrong reasons may cause as much damage as falling into the sin itself. We should be well guided. The sex-is-evil lie is only a statement that misguides.

The Lie: You will always get away with it

You're not sure. When you do something wrong intentionally, or the devil tricks you into doing it, he will also make sure you remember it well for a long time.

Ukeme had sex only twice before marriage. The first time was with an apprentice in his mother's catering business, when he was just fifteen years old. The second time was after he gave his life to Christ at the age of twenty-one also with another apprentice of his mother's, though he regretted it because he had been seduced. The first time he had sex, he hardly enjoyed it. He had tried it because of peer pressure. Shortly after that first experience, he had given his life to Christ and vowed to steer clear of women. He however discovered shortly after the 'ordeal' with Iquo the first apprentice, he started itching and discharging. It wasn't so painful at first, so, he ignored it. Later, when the pain was no longer bearable, he complained to his mother and she took him for a Check-up. Ukeme was discovered with Gonorrhea an STD (sexually transmitted disease). His mother was so disappointed but she grudgingly paid for the available treatment. Though treated the first time, he noticed that from time to time, he had painless discharges and sometimes itching, which he always managed to treat with self-prescribed antibiotics. A few months after Ukeme got married at the age of thirty, his wife, Rosemary, was discovered with Gonorrhea to her surprise. After much research and testing, it was discovered that the bacteria that caused Ukeme's Gonorrhea had developed resistance to the treatments he had been self-administering. Here we have Ukeme and his beautiful wife, both believers, faced with a very destructive STD. Because Rosemary's symptoms showed up late, her reproductive system had been tampered with and affected. To cut a long story short the couple could not have any babies with the infection they both had. It took eight years of intensive, expensive treatments before they were medically cleared with reproductive scars. Eight years of intense treatment, coupled with series of prayer and fasting for God to intervene. Almost ten years after marriage, Rosemary delivered a baby girl, their first.

THE TRUTH

The truth is that only Christ can cleanse us from all sin, and the devil can never be the one to tell you if you'll get away with any sin. Because he doesn't know. All the devil knows is his plans to torture you with thoughts and consequences of your sin. The days of ignorance God winked at but at times, while God is looking away and 'winking' at the sin, gross consequences are following; pregnancy, infection, guilt and fear, to mention a few. You cannot afford to take a risk with the precious gift God has given you. You should not be defiled for your future partner, and yet pretend the slate is clean. Oh yes, God does wink at many of the sins we commit before our rebirth. He forgives and His mercy endures, but we cannot afford to enter the trap of the enemy, especially when we have been warned that what a man sows, he will reap Galatians 6:7 and that the wages of sin is death! Romans 6:23. It may or may not be physical death. It could be death of faith, trust, compassion, body parts, confidence and happiness. I do not intend to scare us but when we have the truth, it will set us free John 8:32. The Lord restores but that is not what should motivate us into sin. Paul asked a crucial question in Romans 6:1 (please study Romans 5 & 6). Shall we continue in sin that grace may abound? May we be free in Jesus' mighty name. Amen.

Chapter 3 - MORE LIES

The Lie: Homosexuality is a personal thing

This is a very deep and terrible lie from the pit of hell. The devil has so penetrated the heart of man with this lie that these days, we see 'gay marriages'. This a terrible perversion and God condemns it vehemently Rom1:26,27.

Lola was a very quiet and decent girl before she met Chris. Chris, a short form of Christiana, was a lesbian! Being a girl, Chris looked for all the ways she could to be a boy. She wore trousers, walked with a bounce, kept her hair low almost skinned and talked tough. To crown it up, she was the daughter of very wealthy parents and a senior student in one of the best girls' boarding schools in the country. Chris was two years senior to Lola and she 'fell in love' with her. Chris devised ways of 'making love' to Lola in odd places (since they didn't have the chance to do this in the dormitory under the steady gaze of others). They met in the school farm, in the dining hall in the middle of the night, in the classrooms when no one was there and even once, in the bathroom. Chris did things that felt wrong to Lola but she responded. Gradually, Lola came to enjoy the sin. When Chris graduated after a year, Lola went ahead and started sleeping with Paula, her classmate. It went from one perversion to the other till Lola finally graduated. She had found herself, seeking love from people of the same sex. In the university she was different, and soon she met those that were her kind. When Lola gave her life to Christ through the ministry of a former lesbian, twelve years later, she had to go back to the beginning. Her psychology was so depraved that at age thirty, as a single woman, she believed God could do a miracle and give her children from a gay marriage! Lola is currently still undergoing therapy and Christian counseling two years after surrendering her life to Christ.

THE TRUTH

The Bible also talks of 'unnatural affection' (2 Tim 3:1-9), reprobate minds seeking evil with their depraved and distorted minds (v.8 – Amplified version), lovers of sensual pleasure and vain amusements (v.4). Often in the Western world we hear of gay preachers, and laws protecting homosexuals. We hear of human rights fighters, debating the homosexual cause. These days, we have celebrities flaunting their perversion in the sight of their maker. Believers and even pastors now seek to 'love the sinner and hate the sin', encouraging brethren to overlook the 'orientation' of the 'gay brethren'. This is evil in the sight of God.

I want to charge and encourage Christians all over the world to withstand these evil laws and rights in the place of prayer. We can only bind them and confuse their languages on our knees because the weapons of our warfare are not carnal but mighty through God to the pulling down of strongholds, casting down imaginations, and every high thing that exalts itself against the knowledge of God, bringing every evil thought into captivity and the obedience of God (2Cor 10:4,5). Homosexuality is a grievous sort of sexual perversion and depravity. The Bible clearly states that marriage and sexual union should be between 'man and wife'. Homosexuality does not only contradict this word of God, it also challenges the command of God to 'be fruitful and multiply' Gen 1:28, and it ridicules the comfort of the word of God that 'children are the heritage of the Lord, the fruit of the womb His reward' (Ps 127:3). To help you hate this sin, remember Sodom and Gomorrah! Genesis 19.

The Lie: Masturbation harms no one

Ekene started masturbating at the age of eight. He never could recall how it all started but he just found himself doing it. At first, he only watched blue films that excited him sexually and then he would have a 'release'. As he grew older, he devised other more exciting means and perfected the act. When he was sixteen, he had his first sexual encounter with a woman. It wasn't as much fun as he had anticipated. However, he wasn't discouraged. He slept with a few other ladies and drew the conclusion that sex alone was better than sex with anyone. Though he continued 'dating and breaking' he held on to his 'solo' act. Ekene finally surrendered his life to Christ and after listening to messages about fornication, considered himself 'safe' with masturbating. However, he discovered that after he masturbates, a deep feeling of guilt and shame comes upon him and he would feel really dirty. When he sought counseling, he confirmed what he had feared: masturbating was as much sex as sex! And he had to stop that too. With a deep sense of repentance, he let go of this dirty act, and sought God to help him stop. It was not easy!

THE TRUTH

Masturbation harms no one but you. Masturbation is a subtle way the devil has used to confuse and contradict the plan and purpose God has for sex. Medical experts have tried to establish that masturbation is healthy. Some others have also excused masturbation as a way of easing sexual tension without fornicating or committing adultery. It has been argued that masturbation is the easy and confident way out of sin. Wrong. This is wrong because masturbation is sinful. Ask yourself this; what is the difference between masturbation and sex? I'll tell you one difference: For sex, you need another human being; for masturbation, you need images, personal stimuli, or instruments. Either way, the goal is to reach an orgasm. Bottom line, sex is still sex!

When masturbating, there must be images in the mind that will help to stimulate the flow. It could be images from films, novels, something you happened upon (maybe someone's nudity, or sex act) or even imaginations about someone you have been seeing around, or even dreamy imaginations of the ideal person, pictured in your mind. These add up to even make masturbation sin. In fact, the Bible sees this sin (evil and lusty imagination) as potently as the very act, Mt. 5:27, 28.

The fact that the word 'masturbation' is not found in the Bible does not excuse this disturbing act. It is enough that the bible frowns at anything outside sex between 'man and his wife'. May God give us a deeper understanding and the grace to overcome this tricky sin in

Jesus' mighty name. Amen. This sin must be tracked down and arrested because it is a secret indulgence. You can boldly say I am a virgin at age 30, but you have been cheating secretly through masturbation. We should be careful. This bad habit can hold someone bound even after marriage and this is very dangerous to healthy sex in marriage. A Christian lady bound by masturbation for over twenty years by the time she was thirty had difficulty after marriage, submitting to her husband in 'bed' and often found sex with him unappealing because she was used to getting the 'same' satisfaction on her own.

The Lie: Abortion is the only solution to a mistake

The abortion debate has become a global one. But despite the publicity given this lie, the devil continues to confuse and defeat women with it.

Debbie was one of over fifty children of a very rich polygamous man. Being a member of such a family, success was paramount to her. She needed to have a home 'of her own', family and wealth so that whenever she visited home for occasions, she would and could show herself off proudly. However, she couldn't. She had a major problem that paralyzed all her efforts in life. She couldn't have a child. Though successful in business, her money meant nothing to her. As a young girl in university, she had dated a nice guy and gotten pregnant for him. With the advice of her friend who boasted of having had three or more abortions, she aborted the pregnancy without second thoughts. She never got pregnant again. After five years of marriage to her first husband, the marriage collapsed because the man wanted a child. The second and third husbands came and went quickly before Debbie, closer to fifty than forty, decided to quit trying. She lives alone today!

THE TRUTH

The word abortion is not really visible in the Bible just like the other words that the devil pertinently uses to tell us lies. However, the sixth commandment includes abortion Exodus 20:13. Even in some countries of the world, Nigeria inclusive, abortion is illegal as it is tantamount to killing (this means that if you are a Nigerian and you abort or aid abortion for someone, you have not only broken the law of God, you have also broken the law of your country). Not only that, abortion is even interrupting God's divine order.

Miriam got married at a very young age, barely eighteen. She got pregnant immediately, and had a baby boy. Two months after her first baby was born, she found herself pregnant again. However, this time around, friends advised her to abort the pregnancy. "Your husband and his family will not be happy with you...it is not medically safe for you..."on and on went the 'evil' counsels. Without seeking the consent of her husband, she aborted the baby. She never got pregnant again after that. Her husband however wanted more children, and took a second wife. The second wife started having children immediately. Miriam comforted herself with her only son. Tragedy struck when the boy was seven years. He had a serious case of measles. The boy died from the sickness. Miriam became a very miserable woman. Instead of two or more children, she grew into old age childless.

I have seen where people 'abort' spontaneously. Medics call it miscarriage. I have also heard a testimony of where God Himself took the pregnancy away. On that occasion, the married woman got pregnant after having five children and she prayed to God to take the pregnancy away, and God did. One day, she was two months pregnant. The next day, she was not pregnant at all – no bleeding, no pain, no signs, just no pregnancy. God can do His miracle any way He wants. Of course, this woman was pregnant for her husband. This is just to tell us that God can have other solutions to your problem.

Uju died at the age of twenty-five. She was a final year student of pharmacy in the university. She had had an unsuccessful operation that caused her death. Uju had had a sixth abortion before her death. It wasn't the abortion that caused her death. It was complications arising from the abortion. The womb ruptured two days after the abortion and she had to be rushed into the theatre. She never came out alive. Not only was a sixth child aborted and murdered, another destiny, a success, a promising future as a pharmacist had also been aborted.

Abortion is a fatal manipulation of the truth, and the repercussion can be so damaging. God is a just God and for every seed sown (even in the days of ignorance) there is a harvest. I am not saying that God doesn't forgive or that He will not wink at the days of our ignorance as His word tells us in Acts 17:30. What I am saying is that if a tree is planted, it will grow under normal circumstances and it is only if we uproot it that it will stop growing. The truth is 'to be fore-warned is to be fore-armed'. Now that you know that it is wrong in the sight of God, and punishable by God, you should repent and not do it again!

Aborting a baby, may sow death, infertility, infection or an ever-present guilt feeling. The bible calls the devil the accuser of brethren Revelations 12:10 and he is always there to remind us of what we did. The danger here is that you don't know the abortion that will seal and stamp you 'BARREN'. You don't know the one that will end up with complications and death. When a child is not doing well, the devil will lie to us that our 'promise child' was the one aborted! I have seen abortion destroy homes and lives through death, inability to have other children, spending fortunes to cure infections and correct mistakes, breeding hatred, and suspicion. One solution that God has to abortion is having the child. There will always be someone, somewhere that God will lead us to for help. Students may lose two years of their academics or even much more but gain a clear conscience before God. And a child is a blessing any day! The Bible asks what will it profit us if we gain the whole world (attention, respect, time) and lose our own soul? Matthew 16:26.

Please note here that if a person got raped, she should report at a clinic or hospital within 48 hours of the incident, or as soon as she can have access to medical care and medical advice on how to prevent likely conception! This advice is not for fornicators, please.

Chapter 4 - CONTEMPORARY LIES

The Lie: I can use what I have to get what I want

This is a pervasive and contemporary lie the devil has used to destroy many young girls. A shocking number of born again Christian girls particularly those in tertiary institutions believe it is their right (maybe even God-given) to use their bodies to acquire their material needs.

Alero had always been complimented for her shapely body. Her legs especially held an attraction that both male and female acquaintances appreciated. Yet she was from a poor family background. Her mother was a seamstress while her father was a retired non-commissioned officer of the Nigerian Army. In the days when Alero was born, life was generally easy for men in uniform. There was free accommodation, feeding and education. Alero's parents had taken full advantage. She was born fourth out of thirteen children. When her father retired, the accommodation was retrieved and he had to rent a two-room apartment for the large family. Gradually, it became clear he couldn't cater for his family and he took the coward's way out of trouble. He began to drink and get aggressive and abusive of his family. He beat his wife up and made her bear all the financial responsibility of the family.

It soon became clear that a serious solution was needed if the children would have good education. Alero, by then a second-year student of the university, decided to fend for herself. Her three older siblings, though in the working class, were already saddled with the responsibility of the remaining nine children who were still at various stages of secondary and primary education. Alero took the easy way out, she explored all the possibilities of her natural endowment. It had begun when a brother asked her out and she poured her needs on him. The speed with which he responded baffled her. But soon after, the young Christian Brother, who was also a student, could not meet all of Alero's needs. It was time for Sister Alero to move on. When another Christian Brother asked for a relationship, Alero turned him down because she did not see any prospect in the relationship. Rather, she went along with a richer brother, who was married.

Alero's relationship with the married man lasted for a few months through which he rented a self-contained apartment for her, thereby moving her out of the hostel. He bought gifts for her and improved her standard of living. In return, she gave herself to him. This relationship was not as innocent as the first one. The man demanded sex, and Alero yielded. Afterall, life was all about give and take.

THE TRUTH

I have seen many young ladies lose their self-value because of this deadly lie. Truth is that men will take advantage of whoever allows them to. Many Aleros end up with one, two, three or several men. A lady I once knew confessed that she was only dating the men to see herself through school. Her father was dead, and her mother was a petty trader. Another one dated just one man who was old enough to be her father. Her father was also dead. She wanted to break off the relationship but the man had bought her a car, rented a flat for her, paid her school fees, and was sponsoring trips abroad for her. She decided that she would end the relationship as soon as she finished her education and moved out of town. That meant she would still date him for another one year since she was in her penultimate year!

To be sincere with ourselves, what do you really have as a girl? Transient beauty that fades. To what purpose did God endow you with the body you have – a female body? What is that need in your life that God cannot give? What do you actually gain when you abuse your body in search of material comfort? We always give excuses: my family is poor; my father is dead; my mother is sick; my father is retired; I need the money; ... and on and on goes the excuses. Take time and answer the questions posed in this paragraph.

A woman of God I appreciate and respect deeply shared her life story in our church. As an unbeliever, she had been completely bought over by this lie. She was what we call a "happening babe" on campus. She changed men as she changed her wardrobe, then she met Jesus. God touched her and she forsook her sinful ways. One fear though plagued her – who would sponsor the rest of her education. She gave up sleeping around and thrust her life into God's hands and He saw her through school. She had thought it was impossible as a young lady to pass through higher institution without at least keeping one man but God surprised her. Though it wasn't easy, He saw her through. Today, she is happily married with children.

God delights in being the Fourth Man in our Fiery Furnace as He was for Shadrach, Meshach and Abednego (Daniel 3). These days, many young Christian ladies who are unfortunate to have sponsors for their education, take up jobs as clerks, salespersons, and even housemaids. Some have been blessed enough to have godparents in the church, who take up their education. Whatever way God does it, He is well able to take care of His own. All you need to do is put your trust in Him. This lie does not apply to girls alone, but also our young men. Patronising "Sugar Daddies" and "Sugar Mummies" is abominable in the sight of God.

The Lie: Condom is an alternative

The campaigns to checkmate the spread of the deadly HIV/AIDS epidemic has unwittingly become an instrument of the evil one to spread an easy to believe lie among our youths – that sex with condom is as good as abstinence. But it is what it is – a great lie.

Ekpedeme loved to play safe. The benefits were tremendous. She took it upon herself to get the condoms so there would be no mistakes. Condom to her was the greatest innovation on earth. No unwanted pregnancies, or unwanted diseases. You could actually eat your cake and have it! It was no wonder to her that when she chose to get married, she got the man of her dreams, and she had a healthy baby within the first year of her marriage. Ekpedeme was in high spirits. She had gotten away with stolen waters! Nothing pastor had talked about sexual sin worked. She had tried it and seen it. All the hullabaloo about danger in committing sex sins had evaded her. She had gotten away with it! Why then the fear?

Shortly before she got married, she had started seeing things; imagining strange evil. At first, she was scared she would die before marriage. Then she started having this fear of not having children. She had nightmares and saw some of her old lovers prevailing over her. Then her husband started suspecting her. They had horrible quarrels over nothing. Somehow Ekpedeme felt vindictive. But she couldn't place her hands on her adversary. When one of her old lovers re-entered her life and demanded for a relationship, she knew she was in trouble. She realized that years of cutting corners with God were finally catching up with her. On this one, she had to come out plain with her husband to get help. It was what her pastor told her when she went for counseling.

THE TRUTH

Condom cannot protect you from the wrath of God. It cannot help you when your partner starts to distrust you. It cannot even help you from the guilt you feel. The truth here is that sex is not only physical, but deeply spiritual. It involves soul mating, and soul tying. Many of us look at the dangers in the physical and forget we are spirit beings. You sleep with someone, and there is a deposit forever. Many people need to deliver themselves from all sorts of souls they have tied themselves to. Don't be deceived by the good values of the 'rubber'. It as much prevents the diseases as it prevents you from the glory of God.

Stay away from the condoms. Stay away from the sin.

Chapter 5 - NEVER TOO LATE

The purpose of this book is to draw our attention to the evils and tactics of the devil and to make us realize that we are targets of his plan. No matter where we turn to, there will always be a lie, waiting to accost us. We must know that the devil has been succeeding tremendously in his work, and it is high time, Christians arose to combat it.

We may not have the means to stop the devil from polluting the world, but we can stop him from destroying us, our children, our neighbours and our friends.

My mother made it clear to me from my university days that she would not be pleased if I ever got pregnant before marriage, but she assured me that if it ever happened, I should not abort and she would take responsibility of the child for me. This did not only give me the said assurance, it made me determine not to do even what will make me get pregnant. We can work with our children and their friends to influence them, and we can work with youths and singles to help them from falling prey to the devil.

Lovina, a young year one university student, just born-again, discovered she had missed her period. When she came for counseling, she was afraid for two reasons. First, she was afraid she was pregnant for her doctor boyfriend. Second, she was afraid that if she was pregnant, her mother would 'kill' her. Apparently, she had gotten pregnant two years before and her mother had ensured she had an abortion, warning her never to get pregnant again. What did we expect from Lovina? After the pregnancy test was found positive, her doctor boyfriend convinced her she had to abort. Without seeking further help from the church, she went ahead and did it but came back with a guilt feeling to 'report' herself for what she had done. At this point, Lovina can be stopped and helped because she desires to repent and change.

A small research carried out amongst a random group of Christians show that the devil is not sleeping and so we shouldn't either. 275 adults were selected, all above sixteen years of age. Amongst these, 154 were married and 121 unmarried.

RESULT OF RESEARCH

154 married people.

Virgins as at the time of marriage

Men: 2.6 %

Women: 12.3%

Not Virgins as at the time of marriage

Men: 43.5%

Women : 38.3%

Inadmissible response – 3.3%

This is very alarming and it shows that less than 20% of those that responded to the questionnaires were able to keep themselves to the marriage bed.

121 Single people.

Virgins

Men: 9.9%

Women: 25.6%

Disvirgined:

Men: 26.5%

Women: 34.7%

Inadmissible response: 3.3%

How many of the 35.5% that are still virgins amongst the singles, will stay till the marriage bed? This is our work. We do not need to look back if we were unfortunate enough to have been deceived by the devil. All we have to do is look forward and determine not to give more

success to the devil. It is not in God's plan that
we are deflowered before marriage, and it is
not His purpose for us to, by our own hands;
remove a gift He allowed into our wombs.
However, it is never too late to yield ourselves
to Him.

Flora had three abortions for her boyfriend.
The three came in quick succession within
a period of two years. Though a born-again
Christian, she had entangled herself with an
unbeliever who had no value for human life.
He convinced her that the foetus was not a
real human being anyway, and took complete
charge. She knew she had offended God and
after the third abortion, despite threats from
her boyfriend to destroy her 'if she left him',
she ended the relationship. She confessed her
sins, and turned from them completely. Today, Flora has a family of her own. To say the
story ended with 'and she lived happily ever
after' will not be truth. As someone who has
aborted before, she still dreams of the babies
she never saw, despite the fact that she now has

other children, yet, God is still working on her
to heal her of every guilt feeling she still battles
with.

Let us get closer to God and let Him lead
us in the way that we should go. We must
not remain sorrowful and guilt-laden in our
mistakes but we must repent and move on,
determined not to allow the devil to gain more
ground with us. The bible says that Godly
sorrow works repentance, 2 Corinthians7:10.
When we repent we start afresh with God and
then move on from there, helping as many
people as we can along the way. Some of our
experiences are sometimes mainly to strength-
en us so that we can strengthen others to keep
moving on.

Chapter 6 - THE SECRET

There are several secret ways to beat the devil to the game. A few will be treated in this passage to help us.

1. Avoiding sex before marriage.

When we are pure before marriage, the problem of abortion will never be ours. So in essence, by being pure before marriage, we are not only pleasing God but also avoiding trouble. Prevention they say is better than cure. Then, how can we prevent this strong urge. When we haven't tried it, it's easier (what you don't know, you don't worry about) but how do we prevent the urge from overwhelming us and drawing us into sin, either as all-time virgins or as regenerate virgins.

a. You must accept and acknowledge that you are peculiar, and that you have very peculiar needs. Some are weak and some are strong. In this acknowledgement, you must discern to what group you belong. How do I react around people of the opposite sex? How do I react to the person I am sexually attracted to? Do I always want to hold, touch, pet, and cuddle, fondle, and receive reciprocal actions? Do I feel I must have sex to be relieved each time I have a sexual urge? You know yourself better than anyone else. Study yourself and be sincere to yourself.

b. Attempt to know the person you are dealing with. If you are in a relationship with someone, be open about yourself and encourage the person to be open also. Don't deceive yourself. If your friend is weak, help him/her by avoiding too much closeness and undue attention to parts of your body and your partner's. 'I have a boil on my thigh' could be an innocent complaint that will turn to an erotic battle.

c. Talk about the things that will take your attention off sex, and also express your momentary feelings to each other. 'I feel funny, let's go for a walk' – is appropriate. Let's go for this or that programme or let's go visiting. Don't hide your feelings and don't feel you can handle them alone. It could bottle up and blow up in your face some day. Don't feel that your partner will look down on you or make you feel cheap. Owning up to a weakness is better than falling victim to sin.

d. Flee every appearance of sexual temptation. The devil does not present himself as the devil. He comes in subtle ways to trick us. If you realize your emotions are getting hard to control or that of your partner's, excuse yourself. Don't think that if we hug, it will bring a release. Hugs lead to touching and caressing, and these lead to kissing and other things.

Don't for once think that you are stronger than the temptation. When you see it coming, excuse yourself don't wait for it to overwhelm you.

e. Seek scriptural and spiritual advice, when you begin to see it as a consistent problem.

f. Pray for yourself and your partner. God is able to save us from all sin so you should commit yourself to him continually.

2. Avoiding other sexual sins that pervert sex within the confines of marriage.

Adultery, homosexuality, and so on are all wrong uses of sex that the bible frowns at; hence we have to know how to avoid indulging ourselves in them. This especially is for those who have been guilty of such sins, and are having difficulty coming out.

a. Admit that you have a problem. The first step to being free is admittance. The bible says that it is with our mouths that confession is made unto salvation Romans 10:10.

b. Admit that you need help, and have a desire to change. It is important to desire to change; otherwise there will be no help. Jesus stands at the door of our hearts, knocking and waiting for a response. He will not force Himself in. Willingness to let go is very important.

c. Be willing to break off all contact with the person(s) or imaginations involved. This may be difficult especially if this one is someone around you (in the office, in church, neighborhood, or in the family) but contact and communication must be severed.

d. Work towards building up for yourself self –concepts that are based on scriptures. Be vocal about calling sin, sin. Don't indulge evil. Be violent about it Matthew 11:12.

e. Seek mature and spiritural counseling and deliverance.

f. Pray for yourself. God hears the cry of the humble and needy. Psalms 9:12; James 4:6; Hebrews 4:16.

3. Some ways Parents/Guardians can help.

a. Build up a healthy home environment for the children. Know and encourage your child and show love. Let the child know the word of God and that they are special to you and to God. Avoid having verbal and physical fights with your spouse before them.

b. Educate the child. Listen to and teach the child. Encourage the child to express him/herself at all times. Let them ask questions freely and provide truthful and simple answers to the questions especially in the area of sex.

c. Avoid every form of abuse, either physical or psychological. Discipline and correct in love, but do not deprive them of basic needs as a means of punishment.

d. Have expectations for the child and let the child know that he/she gives you pleasure (even if it is not obvious) and encourage the best out of the child.

e. Allow them to explore themselves and their environments. When we hold on too rigidly they will sneak out and slip away. Commit them into God's hands and allow Him to take care of them.

f. Identify with your child's peculiarities, difficulties and challenges and stay involved in your child's life. Always give him/her the attention he/she needs.

Finally, prayer is the master key. When we indulge ourselves in the word of God and we give ourselves steadfastly to prayer and fasting, sincerely serving God, some of the challenges will be turned into opportunities Romans 12:9-12.

May God forgive us. May He help us to forgive ourselves. Amen.

Chapter 7 -
CONCLUSION –
FEAR GOD

Let us hear the conclusion of the whole matter. Eccl. 12:13, 14 says fear God, keep His commandments for this is the whole duty of man. So, what about the fear of God? The fear of God is wisdom Job 28:28; and Prov. 4:7 says wisdom is the principal thing so we can deduce from this that the fear of God, is the principal thing.

When I was in the University, we were told by our spiritual 'daddies and mummies' not to do those things we couldn't do publicly before other brethren. I pondered on this. There were a lot of things I could do and say in the presence of brethren but then there were also a number of things I would not do either because it was based on my little understanding of the scriptures or it just was not a decent presentation beyond my bathroom! So, I discarded that theorem. Since I found this 'law' faulty, I sought another that was more practical and I discovered it was the fear of God. And I told myself "anything that I would do, that I will not feel comfortable about, under the steady gaze of my God, then I would not do". It was not easy to keep myself in remembrance of this, but it has been very helpful. This is what kept me mostly through my singles days. I heard a true life story of a brother and sister (call them Isaac and Rebecca) who were in courtship. They were very sure to get married, and so one day, brother Isaac felt a deep urge to taste of the 'good thing' that will soon be his. Sister Rebecca was scared. She was especially particular about someone, anyone seeing them. In order to convince his sweetheart, the brother Isaac ensured that the door lock was secured and the curtains properly drawn. He stood and looked at her in anticipation of the 'love' they were about to share, admiring her beauty and courage. Sister Rebecca sighed and looked at him.

"There is one last curtain you haven't drawn" she told him.

"Which one?" he looked quickly at all the well-drawn curtains.

"The one for the window where God is standing, looking at us" she said. He got the message and remembered that God was also watching. He broke down and apologized.

The relationship was saved. How about when we don't remember God is watching? I also heard of a couple in courtship, who rose up from a bed of fornication, feeling guilty. The brother felt so much guilt that he turned on the sister and accused her of being a witch sent from hell to make him fall. A few minutes earlier in the heat of their affection, she had been the 'love of his life'. The duo never made it to the altar.

Brethren, I challenge us to fear God. The word 'fear' as seen in Eccl. 12:13 means 'yare', a Hebrew word translated to mean 'revere'. The way we revere God every day opens us up to the blessing of the scriptures, and wisdom for daily living. When the question 'what am I to do?' comes up, remember that God is watching. Our God cannot behold iniquity Ps. 66:18 and so we have to remember that if we want God to keep watching us, then iniquity must be far from us. When we fall into error or sin, and we confess and repent, He is faithful and just to forgive us and cleanse us from all unrighteousness 1 John 1:9. but when we go on in sin, we fall into iniquity because iniquity is a persistent sin. God cannot behold iniquity for He is holy, Isaiah 59:2; I Peter 1:16. Do not fear man or what man can do to you. Do not fear sin, for it will destroy you but fear the one who can deliver you from man and sin. Fear God. He has not stopped watching. Even though His grace is sufficient for you, keep on fearing Him. The fear of God is wisdom . . . . Wisdom is the principal thing. IN ALL THY GETTING, GET THE FEAR OF GOD.

REFERENCES

1. LIFEWAY MAGAZINE VOL. 3 NO. 2 APRIL – MAY 2003.

2. THE YOUNG MINISTER'S HANDBOOK BY MIKE MURDOCK.

3. TEEN STUDY BIBLE BY THE ZONDERVAN CORP. © 1993, 1998.

4. CHRISTIAN COUNSELLING. A COMPREHENSIVE GUIDE BY GARY R.COLLINS, Ph.D. REVISED EDITION. © 1998.

5. THE NEW KING JAMES VERSION OF THE BIBLE. THOMAS NELSON, INC. © 2000.

6. THE AMPLIFIED BIBLE BY ZON-DERVAN AND THE LOCKMAN FOUN-DATION. © 1987.

7. STRONG'S EXHAUSTIVE CON-CORDANCE BY JAMES STRONG, S.T. D., L.L.D. BAKER BOOK HOUSE COM-PANY. © 1992.

8. INSPIRATION FROM THE HOLY SPIRIT.

sometimes .... never
....

12. have you aborted before?   Yes
.... No ....

13. if yes, how many times
....

14. how many sex partners have you had?
....

Thank you for sincerely filling out this in-
formation.

Acknowledgments

Special thanks to: Pastor & Mrs. Chuma Chinye, whose constructive and spiritual contribution is spread through the pages of this book; Dr. & Dr. (Mrs) Pat Asuquo; my husband, Pastor Folarin Ogúnyinka; Pastor Paolo Ogbeche; the entire congregation of The Redeemed Christian Church of God, Flourishing Branch, Calabar; members of Federal Ex-Students Christian Association, Calabar Chapter; my constant friend, Onose Adeleye; and all the youths who contributed by administering the questionnaire.

God bless you all.

ARE YOU SAVED?

All that is written in this book may not be of much use to you if you haven't yet given your life to Christ. We cannot overcome the lies by our mere might. We need the one that is greater than the devil to fight for us. The Bible says that greater is He that is in us, than He that is in the world IJohn 4:4. And we wrestle not against flesh and blood but against principalities, against powers, against the rulers of the darkness of this world, against spiritual wickedness in high places Ephesians 6:12.

If you haven't yet given your life to Christ, and you want to do so, please pray this prayer of faith:

Father, I honour you. I praise you and I acknowledge you that you are Lord. I know I am a sinner and I ask that you forgive me all my sins. I want you to be my Lord and personal Saviour. Wash me clean and give me grace to serve you wholly from now on. Come into me heart to reign supreme. In Jesus' name I pray. Amen.

Praise God, you are born again.

Now that you have prayed this prayer of faith, I admonish you to:

• Get a Bible, and read it every day (Start from the first four books of the New Testament to familiarize yourself more with your new Commander-in-Chief, Jesus Christ)

• Pray every day.

• Attend a Living Church

• Introduce yourself to the Pastor and seek further teaching (you can join the foundation class and activity group in church – you are hence making yourself available to work for God)

• Tell others about your salvation.

May God help you in Jesus' name. Amen.

THE NIGERIAN CHILD – MY VISION

Hab. 2:2 Then the LORD answered me and said: "Write the vision And make it plain on tablets, That he may run who reads it.

More than before, it's time for the well-to-do to cater for the less-privileged. Over the past few years, the Lord has laid this burden for THE NIGERIAN CHILD on my heart and I believe it's time to spread the vision. I have a desire to help and to instigate help for THE NIGERIAN CHILD. There are currently five areas of help I have been able to identify.

1. THE MARKET-SCHOOL PROJECT: this vision is aimed at eradicating street

and market hawking in the long run. The strategy is to erect schools in market places where children hawking can take a few hours out to learn and then go back to their jobs. It is a long term project and a highly capital intensive one.

2. THE BREAD AND MILK PROJECT: bread and milk will be given in the morning time to children trekking to school just before school resumes. It can be done once a month, once a week or everyday. Or as rampantly as the provision is available. It is not very capital intensive and as little as N50 or $0.35 (US dollar) can feed a child with bread and warm milk

3. THE UMBRELLA PROJECT: to help alleviate the suffering of children who hawk on the streets (while we work towards eradicating hawking on our streets), by providing umbrellas especially during the rainy season. The umbrellas can also be useful during the scotching hot weathers. Umbrellas of different sizes will be given depending on the size of the

child. Prices of umbrellas range from N350.00 to N500.00 or $2.50 to $3.50 (US dollar).

4. THE SORT-A-CHILD PROJECT: which is aimed at helping at least a child in whatever capacity you can. It can be by paying a sick child's hospital bills, buying food and clothing for a child or paying a child's school fees. It can be as long as a life-time commitment or a one-time affair.

5. THE STUDENT CARE PROJECT: for secondary and tertiary students who can't afford their school fees. The idea is to help through the bob-a-job initiative.

THE NIGERIAN CHILD vision is not another non-governmental, money-spinning organisation. It is service to God and provision for THE NIGERIAN CHILD. It can be done privately or corporately. The important thing is to help a NIGERIAN CHILD.

I beg to challenge EVERY CHURCH IN NIGERIA to adopt the SORT-A-CHILD PROJECT or as the Lord lay it on our hearts.

HELP!

Signed - THE NIGERIAN CHILD

By the same author:
* SISTER MINISTER (Based on true life experiences)
* STRENGTH OF CHARACTER (Devotional & Workbook)
* TO WHERE THE WIND BLEW

ISSUES OF LIFE SERIES: (co-authored)
* SOMEBODY HELP! SHE LOVES MY HUSBAND
* SOMEBODY HELP! HE LOVES MY WIFE

www.ingramcontent.com/pod-product-compliance
Lightning Source LLC
Chambersburg PA
CBHW051636120626
46551CB00014B/2105